Whatever Is Lovely

90-DAY DEVOTIONAL

BroadStreet
PUBLISHING

D1715648

BroadStreet Publishing Group LLC
Racine, Wisconsin, USA
Broadstreetpublishing.com

Whatever Is Lovely: 90-Day Devotional
© 2018 by BroadStreet Publishing

978-1-4245-5664-9

Devotional entries compiled by Michelle Winger.

Design by Chris Garborg | garborgdesign.com
Edited by Michelle Winger | literallyprecise.com

Printed in China.
18 19 20 21 22 23 24   7 6 5 4 3 2 1

Above all else,

guard your heart,

for everything you do

flows from it.

PROVERBS 4:23 NIV

Introduction

We know from Scripture that we should think about things that are lovely, good, and pure. But how do we find this in a world that seems to be unraveling at the seams?

This 90-day devotional will encourage you to spend time with God, experiencing his goodness, and being refreshed in his presence. Let your mind dwell on all that is excellent, and give thanks to your Creator who has blessed you with so much.

Remember the greatness of God today as you fix your eyes on his truth.

Come Away

My beloved speaks and says to me:
"Arise, my love, my beautiful one, and come away,
for behold, the winter is past; the rain is over and gone.
The flowers appear on the earth, the time of singing
has come."

SONG OF SOLOMON 2:10-12 ESV

Some say that romance is dead. It's not for God: the lover of our souls. He desires nothing more than time with his creation!

It can be a little uncomfortable to have his gaze so intently upon us though. We're nothing special, after all! Not beauty queens, academic scholars, or athletic prodigies of any kind. We might not be musical, or crafty, or organized. Our house might be a mess, and we could probably use a manicure.

Do you feel a bit squeamish under such an adoring gaze? There is good news for you! You are, in fact, his beautiful one! And he does, indeed, want to bring you out of the cold winter. He's finished the watering season and it is finally—*finally*—time to rejoice in the season of renewal.

How do you feel under the gaze of the Almighty God? Don't be ashamed; he loves you dearly.

Heavenly Father, I don't know why I feel uncomfortable under your gaze. You love me more than anyone else ever could! Regardless of how unworthy I think I am, I want to rise up and come away with you.

Playing Make-Believe

*I know that there is nothing better for people
than to be happy and to do good while they live.
That each of them may eat and drink,
and find satisfaction in all their toil—
this is the gift of God.*
ECCLESIASTES 3:12-13 NIV

We all played our fair share of make-believe as children, twirling around the room in a fancy dress-up gown or running through the fields with a wild tale alive in our minds. Every child probably had those long summer evenings of chasing fireflies and catching dreams, or playing hide-and-go seek and finding destiny. Our starry-eyed youth took our imaginations on the wildest of journeys as our hearts pounded with the creations of our souls.

Pretending we are someone else, or somewhere else, begins early in childhood and more subtly continues as we age. We still allow imagination to transport us to other places, and other circumstances. Somehow it is easier for us to embrace the wonder of "what if" than the reality of "what is."

There is nothing better than to be happy in your life. Your life is made up of now. Each moment you live, each breath you take, it's right this very second. Treasure your life! Be satisfied with where you are. Satisfaction is living each day as if it were the dream.

What dreams are you still holding on to?
Enjoy the process of getting to those dreams
and remember that God wants your happiness.

Father, as I look back on some of my childhood dreams, I realize that it was nice to dream and it made me feel happy. But today is my reality and I pray that you would help me to see my life as a gift. Stir joy in my heart once again.

Prize of Glory

His Spirit joins with our spirit to affirm that we are God's children. And since we are his children, we are his heirs. In fact, together with Christ we are heirs of God's glory. But if we are to share his glory, we must also share his suffering.

ROMANS 8:16-17 NLT

We are God's children. Scripture confirms this for us, so we know it to be true. As his children, we can rest in the knowledge that we are set to inherit all that is his. While that doesn't exempt us from going through rough patches, the good news is that Scripture also tells us that we get to share in his glory. And that is excellent news indeed.

Glory isn't just something nice like a sunny day or a delicious piece of chocolate. It's downright fabulous. Resplendent beauty and magnificence are just a couple of ways to describe it.

Imagine the most beautiful place you've ever been, or the most amazing moment you've ever experienced. It pales in comparison to the glory of God—and we get to share it! Rejoice in this as you reflect on your day. Though you may experience suffering along the way, sharing in his glory is the best prize you could ever receive.

What are the things that are worrying you most about this season in your life? Reflect on the bigger picture today and set your heart on the future glory.

Lord, give me a good outlook for my day ahead. Thank you for providing me with a different perspective. At times, I approach my day with dread, fear, or anxiety, but I know that ultimately this life goes beyond death—you gave me the reality of eternity. Thank you for that!

Perfect Friend

"Here I am! I stand at the door and knock. If anyone hears my voice and opens the door, I will come in and eat with that person, and they with me."

God created you for relationship with him just as he created Adam and Eve. He delights in your voice, your laughter, and your ideas. He longs to fellowship with you. When life gets difficult, do you run to him with your frustrations?

When you're overwhelmed with sadness or grief, do you carry your pain to him? In the heat of anger or frustration, do you call on him for freedom? He is a friend that offers all of this to us—and more—in mercy and love. He is worthy of our friendship.

The friendship he offers to us is a gift of immeasurable worth. There is no one like him; indeed, there is none as worthy of our fellowship than God Almighty, our Maker and Redeemer. Train your heart to run first to God with your pain, joy, frustration, and excitement. His friendship will never let you down!

How is God better than any friend you could ever have?

God, you are the perfect friend. If I think of all I need in a friendship, I know that I can find it in you. Thank you that your friendship surpasses all of my expectations.

Walk Steady

Direct my footsteps according to your word;
let no sin rule over me.
PSALM 119:133 NIV

What is it about high heels? Every family album contains a photo of an adorable toddler attempting to walk in Mama's shoes, and every woman remembers her first wobbly attempt to appear graceful in that first pair of pumps. How did she make it look so easy, so elegant?

Most of us also have a memory of a not-so-graceful stumble or even a twisted ankle; yet, somehow the stiletto retains its appeal. Who hasn't relied on the steady arm of an escort or companion in far more sensible footwear?

Walking with Jesus is a little like learning to walk in four-inch heels. Others make it look so easy, gliding along apparently sinless while we feel shaky and uncertain, prone to stumble at any moment. Will we take a wrong step? Fall flat on our faces? (Do anyone else's feet hurt?)

In which aspect of your walk do you feel the most steady and certain? The least? Share your confidence and your concerns with the Savior, and invite him to lead you in both.

I lean on your strong arm today, my Savior; steady me and direct my steps.

Melody of Worship

God's splendor is a tale that is told;
his testament is written in the stars.
Space itself speaks his story every day
through the marvels of the heavens.
His truth is on tour in a starry-vault of the sky,
showing his skill in creation's craftsmanship
PSALM 19:1-4 TPT

Have you ever felt the song of your heart praising the Lord? No words may come, no verses, no chorus, and yet your very being feels as though it may burst from the music inside you. You are not alone. Even the very heavens praise God in this way!

The Bible tells us that without words, and without even the slightest sound, the skies burst forth in a song of praise for the glory of God. Isn't that an amazing picture? Can't you just envision an orchestra above you?

Break forth into your song. Allow your heart to feel the words, even if you cannot fully form them. Give

God all your praises today. He is so deserving of them. Let your heart be a celebration of your love for Jesus Christ. Give in to the melody of worship inside you.

Picture all of creation worshiping God the way he deserves to be worshiped. Thank him for his goodness to you throughout your life.

*What song is on your heart right now?
Worship God with your song now.*

Heavenly Father, the heavens declare your majesty. As I think about the sun, moon, and stars, may I recognize your voice in your creation, calling me, beckoning me to join in the beauty of the song that they sing. I worship you today. My heart is full of your splendor, and I want that to spill out onto my day.

Follow the Arrow

Your ears shall hear a word behind you, saying,
"This is the way, walk in it,"
Whenever you turn to the right hand
or whenever you turn to the left."
ISAIAH 30:21 NKJV

Decisions, decisions. It seems a week never goes by without our needing to make at least one important choice. Whether job related, relationship motivated, or something as seemingly innocent as how to spend a free Friday, wouldn't it be nice to have an arrow pointing us in the right direction—especially if we are in danger of making a wrong turn?

According to God's Word, we have exactly that. When we truly desire to walk the path God sets us on, and when we earnestly seek his voice, he promises to lead us in the right direction.

God's ever-present Spirit is right with you, ready to put you back on the path each time you wander off.

Consider the decisions before you right now. Who are you turning to for guidance? Lay your options before God, and then listen for his voice.

God, I come to you today and ask for your wisdom. I want to be led by you. You know the path that is best suited to fulfill your plan for my life. Help me to be obedient to you as you show me which way to go.

Glorious

*On the glorious splendor of your majesty,
and on your wondrous works,
I will meditate.*
PSALM 145:5 NRSV

Leaves changing from green to orange to red.
Gently falling snow. A rainbow-colored sunrise.
A sprout of newness in the dirt. The smell of
freshly cut grass. The rustling of leaves in the trees.
The smell of a pine tree. Billowy, moving clouds.
Sunshine kissing your cheeks. It is amazing that
our Creator would make all this for us to enjoy. It's
glorious, really.

Days often go by without us stopping to notice
the wonder around us. We forget to slow down.
We ignore this incredibly beautiful world that God
made for us to explore and enjoy.

Can you make time today to slow down, take a walk outside, and soak in God's presence that's all around you: in the beauty of the sunrise, in the gentle wind blowing through the trees, in the fragrance of a flower in bloom. It is amazing what a walk with a friend, a run through the woods, or the feel of bare feet on grass can do for your soul. Try to make that happen before the day ends.

Can you take time to get outside and enjoy all that God has created?

Creator God, give me an opportunity today to see your glory in your creation. Help me to stop in amazement at the beauty you have put into your world. Help me to discipline myself to get outside and notice the world around me. Thank you that your hidden glory is revealed when I take the time to consider the beauty of nature.

The Writing on the Wall

I will be careful to live an innocent life.
When will you come to me?
I will live an innocent life in my house.
I will not look at anything wicked.
I hate those who turn against you;
they will not be found near me.
Let those who want to do wrong stay away from me;
I will have nothing to do with evil.
PSALM 101:2-4 NCV

What types of messages do we allow to enter our homes on a daily basis through television, social media, internet, magazines, smartphones, or even our own conversations? Do we take the time to really ponder and evaluate the ideas that we absorb even sub-consciously?

Let the messages in your home be messages of godliness. Let your loved ones see and hear the words of life and truth above those of sin and death.

Choose carefully the words and images that enter your home and your heart.

Print some of your favorite verses out and hang them on your walls.

Holy Spirit, you are my greatest ally when determining which messages I should or should not allow into my home. Help me to listen to your prompting, and not ignore you when you gently tell me that something isn't healthy for my spirit.

Joyous Journey

Consider it pure joy, my brothers and sisters, whenever you face trials of many kinds, because you know that the testing of your faith produces perseverance. Let perseverance finish its work so that you may be mature and complete, not lacking anything.
JAMES 1:2-4 NIV

There is great joy in the journey: in the mundane details, in the difficult times, in the confusing moments, and in the tears. There is so much joy to be found in the quiet and in the noise.

Pity parties and comparisons create a direct path for the enemy to steal our joy. There is hope in Jesus and the gift of little joy-filled moments. They come in varying forms: sunshine rays pouring in the windows, a nice person at the check-out counter, a turn-the-radio-as-high-as-it-can-go kind of song, a dance party in the living room, or the taste of a delicious meal after a long day.

There's a journey of joy in waking up every day knowing it's another day to breathe in the fresh air, head to dinner with a girlfriend, or grab coffee with a co-worker. Find joy in the moment, whatever the moment is.

What do you have to be joyful about?
Spend time dwelling on those things.

God, give me joy in whatever I do today, whether it is mundane or exciting. Help me to get my jobs done with a heart full of joy. Help me to create joy with the people around me. Thank you for a day in which I could experience moments of joy. Allow those moments to become more and more frequent, even when things are hard. Help me to be a person that is happy not because of my circumstances, but because I have assurance of your grace and redemption in my life.

Adam was not the one deceived; it was the woman
who was deceived and became a sinner.
1 TIMOTHY 2:14 NIV

Eve, the mother of all, changed humanity forever when she made one fatal decision to venture outside God's boundaries. When she took a bite of the forbidden fruit, she did more than just give in to her own desire for pleasure, she opened the door of sin to every generation that would follow after her.

Eve's key mistake was that she doubted the goodness of God. The serpent knew he could penetrate a woman's mind with well-spoken words, and he convinced Eve that God was withholding something from her. As she believed that God was depriving her, she also believed that God wasn't good after all—that he didn't have her best interest at heart.

The moment Eve stopped believing God was good was the moment that temptation overcame her. Continue to believe that God himself is good. Keep that truth deep in your heart and at the forefront of your mind.

How often do you doubt the goodness of God? Do you wonder if the boundaries he's put in place are really necessary or right? Do you doubt that God really cares about the details of your life?

I choose to remember today, God, that you are good, and that I can trust you completely

Fully Alive

When you follow the revelation of the Word,
heaven's bliss fills your soul.
PROVERBS 29:18 TPT

Everyday living can suck the life right out of us.
Somewhere in the middle of being stuck in traffic,
sweeping floors, and brushing our teeth, we can
forget to be alive.

Without a reason for life, without purpose, we
perish. We falter. We lose our way. We lose hope.
We begin to casually exist instead of breathing in
the reverence of a fully alive life. We need to re-cast
vision for ourselves daily.

What does it mean to be alive, rather than just to live? Not to only exist in life, but to know it, to understand it, to experience it—to live it. What would it be like? Freefalling from an airplane. Running through the grass barefoot with sun on your face. Bringing babies into the world, screaming and strong with power and life. What would it be like if we lived each moment in the spirit of those fully alive moments?

What do you need God to breathe life back into?

Jesus, thank you for filling my soul with your hope and your wonder. Help me to face today as a person who is aware of being fully alive in you. Thank you that you can breathe new life into me even now. Thank you for giving me hope, joy, and peace in the middle of all the other things.

The Cost of Sacrifice

However, the king said to Araunah, "No, but I will surely buy it from you for a price, for I will not offer burnt offerings to the Lord my God which cost me nothing." So David bought the threshing floor and the oxen for fifty shekels of silver.

2 SAMUEL 24:24 NASB

What are you not doing right now because of fear? Are there things you are keeping quiet about simply because you're afraid? Are there steps forward that you aren't taking because you're frightened about what may happen if you do? Are there stirrings in your heart that you're neglecting because you're afraid of how you may be criticized?

In the Bible, when God announced what he was about to do in someone's life, he often began it with the words, "Do not fear." He knew we would worry. He knew we would list the cons and stress over the details, and he said don't.

Trust in the goodness of God's love and allow that to push out any fear that is attempting to rob you of experiencing life.

> *What are you holding back from God? In light of what his death cost him, is there really a price too high for your sacrifice to him?*

Jesus, thank you for dying on the cross and paying the price for my life—not for my money or for my talents. You don't just want the parts of me that others see, you want the secret, hidden part of my heart. Help me to openly show that to you, knowing that you can see it anyway.

No More Thirst

"Never again will they hunger;
never again will they thirst.
The sun will not beat down on them,
nor any scorching heat.
For the Lamb at the center of the throne
will be their shepherd;
he will lead them to springs of living water.
And God will wipe away every tear from their eyes."
REVELATION 7:16-17 NIV

Imagine a marathon with no water stops. A sideline with no giant cooler for the team. Immediately, we picture athletes dropping from dehydration and exhaustion. It's unthinkable.

What is the most thirsty you've ever been? How wonderful did those first few sips taste when your thirst was finally quenched? Perhaps today is one of those days where you feel spiritually dry. Maybe you are working through something in your relationship or workplace and you don't have the creativity, time, or energy to put into it.

One of Jesus' most audacious promises is to take away our thirst. It's extraordinary. He will be all we need, he tells us. Go back to your image of the marathon, and picture yourself running strong, completely free from thirst or pain. Ask the Holy Spirit to reveal what this might look like in your life today.

What needs can Jesus meet? Thank God for the incredible promise of living water to come.

God, thank you that you will provide me with all my spiritual needs. When I am hungry, you will feed me. When I am thirsty, you will provide me with water. You are a God that takes care of me. Wipe away my tears that have come from the pain of hard work. Thank you that while I am running through life, you are there to sustain me with your living water.

You Are Cherished

I am convinced that neither death nor life, neither angels nor demons, neither the present nor the future, nor any powers, neither height nor depth, nor anything else in all creation, will be able to separate us from the love of God that is in Christ Jesus our Lord.
ROMANS 8:38-39 NIV

What feeling really compares to knowing someone has run through the rain, cancelled an international flight, driven all night—for you? Even if we've never experienced it, we've imagined it in our hearts.

Maybe we've had the realization that we, too, would move heaven and earth for the one we love the most. Whether husband, child, parent, sibling, or dear friend, to love and be loved deeply just may be the best feeling there is.

How much love you have given or received is a mere sampling of the way Jesus feels about you.

Let the incredible words above wash over you as you realize there is nothing—absolutely nothing—Jesus wouldn't do for you.

Father, thank you for showing me that I am cherished, loved beyond reason or measure. You really can move heaven and earth, and you would do so in a heartbeat—for me.

In Times of Doubt

God you are near me always, so close to me;
every one of your commands reveals truth.
I've known all along how true and unchanging
is every word you speak, established forever!
PSALM 119:151-152 TPT

The sun will set tonight; it will rise tomorrow. This is truth. We have no reason to doubt what we've witnessed every day of our lives. But when experience tells us otherwise, or perhaps we have no experience to go on, doubts creep in. It's going to snow tomorrow. "I doubt that," we say.

When someone we trust says they'll be there for us, we have faith in their words. Someone who has repeatedly let us down can make the same promise, but we remain uncertain until they've shown up and proven themselves.

Do you feel unsettled today? God wants to erase your doubt and he will; you only need to have faith. God's truth is unchanging. It is sure as the sun that rose this morning and will set tonight.

> *Examine your prayer life. Do you trust God,*
> *or do you doubt his promises to you? Why?*
> *Share your heart openly with him,*
> *and ask him for unwavering faith.*

God, you are near me always; you are so close to me. Thank you that every one of your commands reveals truth. I have faith in your words. Others may let me down. Sometimes I don't even keep true to my word. But your words are true and unchanging! Let me trust in your truth as I go into my day.

A "Yes" Faith

Abram believed the Lord. And the Lord accepted Abram's faith, and that faith made him right with God.
GENESIS 15:6 NCV

Have you ever stepped out and said yes to something crazy for God? You followed him into the middle of the ocean and trusted him to keep you afloat. Stepping out in faith isn't easy. In fact, it's messy. It's a lot of wondering what you're doing, and why you're doing it. Of closing your eyes and begging God to remind you of the things he placed on your heart when he originally gave you the vision.

When you stand in the truth that you have obeyed, it doesn't really matter how everything looks or feels. What matters is that you were obedient. You believed what God was telling you.

Stepping out in faith is about boldly facing your harshest critics and telling them you're not sure if everything will work out. It's being at peace in total chaos. It's putting yourself out there and wondering if you'll live up to expectation. It's wondering if you have anything to offer after all.

If God is asking you to do something that terrifies you, step out in faith. Obey him. Believe him. It will be worth it.

God, there is peace in obedience—peace that even when I'm criticized, laughed at, and misunderstood, you are pleased. Everything else fades away in light of that awesome reality.

Trust the Light

"I am the light of the world. Whoever follows me will not walk in darkness, but will have the light of life."
JOHN 8:12 ESV

Imagine yourself in total darkness, perhaps a wilderness camping trip (or a power failure at a nice hotel if that's more your speed). It's the middle of the night, and you must find your way back to camp. Turn on your flashlight. Though it only illuminates a few steps at a time, it's enough to keep moving. Each step forward lights more of the way, and eventually, you see your destination.

Our faith walk is very much like needing a flashlight to light our step. Most of the time, we can't see where we're headed. Although just a few steps ahead is all we can make out for certain, we trust the path the light reveals.

Jesus is our light. He shows us just what we need to see to put one foot forward at a time. Ask him to help you ignore the unseen and trust the light. Even though the night takes away the sun, you can be sure that it will rise again in the morning. Rest tonight in the assurance that Jesus always lights the way.

What do you need God to illuminate for you now?

Jesus, give me enough light to see the next step. I am ready to move forward in you and so I ask for your revelation and wisdom of where to go next. I ask you to light the way for me. Guide my every step so that I no longer walk in darkness.

Appetite

"No one can serve two masters; for a slave will either hate the one and love the other, or be devoted to the one and despise the other. You cannot serve God and wealth."

MATTHEW 6:24 NRSV

Appetite is a funny thing. Our bodies have the ability to communicate hunger to our brains, and our brains then cause us to seek out a solution to the problem. When we are genuinely hungry, we look for food that will fill our stomachs and quiet our hunger.

Our souls have appetites also, but we so easily fill our time and energy with the world's entertainment. We fill ourselves up with things that will never be able to satisfy and leave little room for the only one who can.

There is a throne in your heart upon which only one master can sit—and you must choose wisely who will take residence there.

Will you allow your life to be ruled by the pursuit of things which will never last, or will you accept nothing less than eternal stock for your life's investment?

God, I want you to be on the throne of my heart. I want to be ruled by the pursuit of eternal life with you.

Finding Peace

*You will keep in perfect peace
all who trust in you,
all whose thoughts are fixed on you!*
ISAIAH 26:3 NLT

What does chaos look like in your world? Crazy work deadlines, over-scheduled activities, long to-do lists and short hours? All the above? How about peace? What does that look like?

Most of us immediately picture having gotten away, whether to the master bathroom tub or a sunny beach. It's quiet. Serene. The trouble with that image, lovely as it is, is that it's fleeting. We can't live in our bathtubs or in Fiji, so our best bet is to seek out peace right in the middle of our chaos. Guess what? We can have it. Jesus promises peace to all who put him first.

How appealing is it to imagine being unmoved by the stresses in your life? Is it easy or difficult for you to imagine claiming this promise for yourself? Ask Jesus to grant you true peace; fix your thoughts on him and watch the rest of the world fade away. When it tries to sneak back in, ask him again.

What are you burdened by right now? Fix your eyes on Jesus and allow him to bring peace into that situation.

God, I fix my eyes on you because I know that is the only way that I will find peace in my crazy world today. Bring peace despite everything that will go on around me today. True peace is knowing that you care about me, and that you care about my eternal salvation. I can rest in the knowledge that my eternity is secure. Let that be enough for me.

No Condemnation

Straightening up, Jesus said to her, "Woman, where are they? Did no one condemn you?" She said, "No one, Lord." And Jesus said, "I do not condemn you either. Go. From now on sin no more."
JOHN 8:10-11 NASB

Most of us know the story of the woman caught in adultery. One of the intriguing moments was when Jesus was questioned about whether or not the woman should be stoned. His response is to stoop down and start writing in the dirt. Jesus' action of stooping in the dirt literally defines one interpretation of the word *grace*.

As they all stood casting judgement, Jesus removed himself from the accusers, stooping low and occupying himself elsewhere. It spoke volumes about his lack of participation in the crowd's judgement. Because of Jesus' distraction, the eyes of the onlookers were drawn off the woman, perhaps lifting a portion of her shame. With their attention focused on Jesus, he said the words that saved the woman's life: "Let him who has never sinned cast the first stone." One by one, the accusers walked away.

Jesus was the only one qualified to stone the adulterous woman. This is a beautiful foreshadowing of the redemption he later brought to all sinners.

Jesus is the only one qualified to condemn you, and he chose to condemn himself instead. You are free and clean because of the grace of Jesus Christ.

Jesus, that you extend your grace to me time and time again blows my mind. I cannot fathom everything that you went through to make me clean and whole. Thank you for not condemning me and for setting me free.

Lifting the Veil

Whenever anyone turns to the Lord, the veil is taken away. Now the Lord is the Spirit, and where the Spirit of the Lord is, there is freedom. And we all, who with unveiled faces contemplate the Lord's glory, are being transformed into his image with ever-increasing glory, which comes from the Lord, who is the Spirit.
2 CORINTHIANS 3:16-18 NIV

Even when we accept Christ as our Savior, there is often a wall that we put up in our hearts. We strive to love him with every fiber of our being, but there can be failure to give him all of us. It's as if the most human part of us feels that by maintaining that last bit of space, we protect ourselves and are free to be who we'd rather be.

True freedom is experienced when we give up, give in, and give ourselves over completely. He wants to take away the veil that prevents us from fully seeing all the beauty that he has in store for us.

Pray that your veil will be lifted—that the last piece of you that may be resisting his Spirit will be given to him today. You are made in his image, and as he lifts the veil from your eyes, allow yourself to be a representative of his grace and love. Experience the freedom that is his glory!

Who is in your life that needs the veil lifted from their eyes? Can you pray for them now?

God, reveal the truth of your Word to me. Thank you that my veil has been lifted and I now see the freedom that I have in you. I have freedom from sin and darkness. There are people in my life who need to see this as well. As I live in your freedom, let your light be revealed to those around me who are still in darkness.

Continual Praise

I will praise the LORD at all times;
his praise is always on my lips.
PSALM 34:1 NCV

It's relatively easy to sing God's praises when all is going well in our lives: when he blesses us with something we asked for, when he heals us, or when he directly answers a prayer. We naturally turn and give him praise and glory for good things. What about when things aren't going well? What about in dry times, painful times, or times of waiting?

Do we only praise God for something after he's given it, or do we praise him ahead of time in faith, knowing that he will always be good no matter what happens?

We should look at all difficulties in life as miracles waiting to happen—chances for God to show his goodness and bring us closer to his heart.

Choose today to have praise readily on your lips instead of complaint. Whenever you feel discontentment or frustration, replace it with praise.

Father, I choose to focus on your goodness today. I know this will increase my joy and lessen the pain of the hardships I am enduring. Give me strength to continue to praise you.

Eternal Fountains

"Whoever drinks of the water that I will give him shall never thirst; but the water that I will give him will become in him a well of water springing up to eternal life."
JOHN 4:14 NASB

We take it for granted that when we turn on a faucet, water will come out. If we need something to drink, we can quench our thirst easily. In Jesus' day, however, people (usually women) had to get their water from the well that was often situated quite some distance away from their homes. It was a necessary daily task that provided for the family's needs.

Imagine being offered water that would last forever. This is what Jesus presented to the woman at the well. She would never have to make the trip again in the heat of the day. Jesus compared her desire with a spiritual desire: just as the well was a source for physical life, he was the source for eternal life.

You have received Jesus as the source for your life. Not only does he say that he will provide you with everlasting water, but he says that his water will be like a fountain, springing up. Are you thankful for the eternal life that Jesus has placed within you? As you get ready to go to sleep, remember to draw from him as your source of life.

How is Jesus refreshing your soul right now?

Thank you, Jesus, for your living water that never runs out. I choose to drink from that everlasting stream today! When I am tired, refresh my soul with your love. Give me a peace as I rest so each morning when I wake up, I am ready to drink from your living water again.

Love that Is Felt

*"These people come near to me with their mouth
and honor me with their lips,
but their hearts are far from me.
Their worship of me is based on merely human rules
they have been taught."*
ISAIAH 29:13 NIV

Think about the most romantic movie you've ever seen. Two beautiful people portray an even more beautiful love on the silver screen, taking your heart on a romantic adventure as they play out passion right before your eyes.

Behind the camera, do those two people really feel that love? They are actors. They are good at what they do. They can make that love story look so very real.

Is love really love when given outwardly but not felt inwardly? Even though it may look to everyone around you that you are passionately in love, if that love is not genuine in your heart, then it's not love at all.

> *If our worship is borne out of true love and intimacy, it will go much further than the outward displays of affection.*

God, your love permeates my heart and my life. I don't want to just look like someone in love, I want to actually be someone who is in love with you.

Truly Special

*You are a chosen people, a royal priesthood, a holy
nation, God's special possession, that you may declare
the praises of him who called you out of darkness
into his wonderful light. Once you were not a people,
but now you are the people of God; once you had not
received mercy, but now you have received mercy.*
1 PETER 2:9-10 NIV

We all want to believe that we are special. Most of
us grow up being told that we are, and it feels good
to believe it. But over time, we look around us and
realize that, really, we are just like everyone else.
Doubt begins to creep in, making us second guess
ourselves and damaging our self-confidence.

Long before you were even a wisp in your mother's
womb, you were set aside and marked as special.
You were chosen to be God's special possession,
and that's pretty amazing. Revel in that knowledge
this evening. He is calling you out of the darkness of
the ordinary, and bringing you into the light of the
extraordinary.

God picked you. He loves you. He wants you. Trust in that and let it change the way you think about yourself.

> *How did God shine his light into your heart? Be thankful that you now experience his mercy each day.*

God, help me to accept that I am special and chosen today. Give me confidence that I can make an influence in this world even today, because you have chosen me to be in this place for a purpose. Thank you for your mercy that can cover any wrongdoing in my day and start me afresh for tomorrow.

Giving Thanks

Open for me the Temple gates.
Then I will come in and thank the Lord.
This is the Lord's gate;
only those who are good may enter through it.
PSALM 118:19-20 NCV

What happens in our souls when we say thank you to God? When we consecrate a passing second by breathing gratitude into it? What happens to our very being when we acknowledge the weight and glory of even the most insignificant gift?

With each moment of paused reflection, each thank-filled statement, we are set free. Set free from negativity. Set free from dark thoughts of death, pain, suffering, and ugliness. We enter his gates with thanksgiving. We enter his holy place. We walk directly through the door he created.

To walk in thanksgiving is to walk right into God's presence.

> *Practice saying thank you today—knowing that through your thankfulness, you will usher yourself into the presence of God.*

God, this season of thanksgiving has a way of taking my heart and righting it. It opens my eyes to wonder and splendor in casual moments. It puts things into perspective and restores triumph to my defeated soul. Thank you!

Rest Secure

I keep the Lord always before me;
because he is at my right hand, I shall not be moved.
Therefore my heart is glad, and my soul rejoices;
my body also rests secure.
PSALM 16:8-9 NRSV

No matter where you are, God is there also. While there may be times when we ache to hide from him in our shame, he is a constant presence. The beautiful thing about his omnipresence is that we have a steady and consistent companion who is always ready to help in times of trouble.

We have no reason to fear the things that the world may throw our way. You might be involved in conflict today, or feel the pressures of life closing in. Perhaps you have to comfort someone, or maybe you are frustrated with how the day is beginning.

Let God be your refuge. Nothing is too big or too small for him! Even in your darkest hours, you can know true joy because he is your guardian. Take your cares and distress, and cast them upon him, because he can handle it. Rest secure in him.

Are you asking for his help in times of worry and woe, or are you turning inward to try to solve your problems?

I'm not sure what today is going to bring me, Lord, but I know you are at my right hand and I don't have to worry about it. Give me gladness throughout the day. When I face stress, I don't often know where to turn. I forget that you are beside me and want to help. Let me be more aware of your Holy Spirit so that I can overcome my fears and troubles.

Rejoice, Pray, Thank

Rejoice always; pray without ceasing; in everything give thanks; for this is God's will for you in Christ Jesus.
1 Thessalonians 5:16-18 nasb

It is easy for us to get weighed down with the negative things in this world. Our lives, and the lives of those around us, are full of troubles that make us weary. Some days it can be difficult to find joy in the midst of our own chaos.

We wonder what God's will is, especially in the hardships. We can't see his master plan, but feel as though if we could, maybe we could make it through. We wonder what God wants us to do in the midst of our difficulties.

These three things: constant rejoicing, prayer, and thanksgiving are the formula for doing God's will in our lives.

Throughout the day, think about what you're thankful for.

God, I rejoice continually in what you have done for me. I want to thank you intentionally for your blessings today.

Kindness Defined

You gave me life and showed me kindness,
and in your providence watched over my spirit.
JOB 10:12 NIV

Kindness. It's an attribute so important to God that he listed it among the fruit of the spirit (along with some other pretty good ones: love, joy, peace, patience, goodness, faithfulness, gentleness, and self-control). But what does it really mean? Is it just being friendly to others? Being nice?

The Bible talks about kindness quite a lot. Even Job, in his misery, recognized how generous and considerate the Lord was of him. When wave after wave of heartbreak took over Job, he still saw God's kindness.

True kindness is defined as being more than that. It's also being generous and considerate. It's a choice we make each day. Are you choosing kindness in your daily life? Are you going beyond just being friendly and being generous? Look for ways in which you can be considerate of others today.

Who can you show kindness to this week?

Lord, open my eyes to the needs of others and show me ways I can be compassionate and kind today. I don't always acknowledge that you are good to me, but I know that you gave me this life and that you are watching over me. Help me to show kindness to others.

Sacrifice of Thanksgiving

Offer to God a sacrifice of thanksgiving
Call upon Me in the day of trouble;
I shall rescue you, and you will honor Me.
PSALM 50:14-15 NASB

The Israelites in the Old Testament had a complicated list of rituals and sacrifices to follow. Among the five special offerings, one was the peace offering, or the sacrifice of thanksgiving. God asked that an animal without defect be offered to him from a heart that was full of gratitude for his grace. When Jesus came, the old requirements were replaced by the new so that our worship could be an expression of our hearts directly through our lips.

It's not always easy to be thankful. In times of great difficulty when everything in the natural screams "I don't like this!" gratitude comes at great sacrifice. It is a denial of the natural response, dying to one's own preference, and in submission saying, "God, your way is best and I thank you."

Having a grateful heart gives us the privilege of calling on God in our day of trouble and the assurance of his deliverance.

> *How can you offer God your sacrifice of praise today?*

Lord, today I want to say thanks for being my God and for the grace you show me each day. As I call out to you, I know you will be my deliverer and get all the glory in the process!

Forever Fashion

As God's chosen people, holy and dearly loved, clothe
yourselves with compassion, kindness, humility,
gentleness and patience.
COLOSSIANS 3:12 NIV

Fashion comes and goes. It can be really fun to see
what's new in stores each season, finding pieces
that update our look and wardrobe. There's nothing
quite like the feeling of finding an item that makes
us feel great every time we put it on—that one
thing we knew was "it" when we saw it in the store.

Fashion is fun, but God calls us to clothe ourselves in
something even better than the latest look off the
runway. He wants us to get dressed in something
that will make us feel even better than our favorite
sweater or a great pair of heels. We are to be clothed
in beautiful character traits that emulate Jesus Christ.

What are you wearing today? Are you all dressed up in compassion? Have you covered yourself with a dose of humility? Is gentleness draped around you, and patience your perfume? Trends in fashion may come and go, but these clothes never goes out of style. Wear them proudly today.

> *What attribute of the Spirit do you need to clothe yourself in right now?*

Lord, let me clothe myself with compassion, kindness, humility, gentleness, and patience today. Guide me to live in these gifts of the Spirit each day. Thank you that you don't care much about what I wear externally. As I read more from your Scriptures each day, I pray that you would teach me how to live by your Spirit so I can be clothed in your beauty.

Beautiful Girlhood

Let their flesh be renewed like a child's;
let them be restored as in the days of their youth'—
then that person can pray to God
and find favor with him,
they will see God's face and shout for joy;
he will restore them to full well-being.
JOB 33:25-26 NIV

Close your eyes for a moment and think back to when you were a little girl. Do you see her? What is she like? Excitable? Passionate? Quiet? Shy?

Remember for a moment what it was like to be that little girl: caring nothing of dirty hands or mussed-up hair. Caring only for that moment—the fleeting moment of freedom and unpredictability. A girl who can lose herself in make believe and dreams. A girl who knows how to dance wildly and run freely. A girl who knows full well the arts of day dreaming and wild flower picking.

That little girl grew up quickly, didn't she? Responsibility eventually overtakes carefree spontaneity. Reality drowns out limitless dreams. Restoration of full well-being can be ours! Doesn't that sound just like childhood? Beloved, God can restore to you what's been lost.

> *What life has threatened to strip from you, God can restore and reshape.*

God, I choose to forget today about the things which never really mattered all that much, and I remember instead what it is to breathe life in my lungs. Thank you for each breath.

Glory Origin

In your glory and grandeur go forth in victory!
Through your faithfulness and meekness
the cause of truth and justice will stand.
Awe-inspiring miracles are accomplished
by your power,
leaving everyone dazed and astonished!
PSALM 45:4 TPT

When we achieve great things, it can be easy to forget where our successes came from. "I worked so hard," we tell ourselves. "I did so much to earn this!" There is nothing wrong with climbing the ladder of success, whatever that is to us, but when we neglect to give the honor to God for all our achievements, we lose sight of the victory itself.

Have you thanked the Lord for what you've achieved lately? He wants us to be successful in our endeavors, but he also wants us to remember where that success came from. We need to remember to humble ourselves in the midst of our triumphs.

We should do everything for the glory of God. He is the one who gives us all that we have. Make that your goal today. While you slay those dragons, take some time to praise God. Go ahead and go for the gold, but give the glory to him, remaining humble all the while.

> *What gifts has God blessed you with to get you to where you are now? Thank him for giving them to you.*

God, thank you for the many gifts that you have given me—even just the ability to sit here right now and read something uplifting. I owe my wonderful life to you. Some days I don't feel that proud of myself, but the fact that I made it through another day of work, family life, or school means that I am using the gifts that you have given me. Thank you.

Troubled Heart

*"Peace I leave with you; my peace I give you.
I do not give to you as the world gives.
Do not let your hearts be troubled
and do not be afraid."*
JOHN 14:27 NIV

I can't get a moment's peace. Sound familiar? We all go through seasons where it seems every corner hides a new challenge to our serenity, assuming we've actually achieved any semblance of serenity in the first place. Why is it so hard to find peace in this world? Because we're looking *in this world*.

After his resurrection, before Jesus ascended into heaven, he left his disciples with something they'd never had before: peace. More specifically, he gave them his peace, a gift not of this world.

Whatever the world can offer us can also be taken from us. Any security, happiness, or temporary reprieve from suffering is just that: temporary. Only the things of heaven are permanent and cannot be taken away.

"Do not let your heart be troubled," Jesus tells us. This means we have a choice. Share the things with him that threaten your peace, and then remember they have no hold on you.

**God, I am yours, and your peace is mine.
Thank you.**

All of You

When the Pharisees heard that he had silenced the Sadducees with his reply, they met together to question him again. One of them, an expert in religious law, tried to trap him with this question: "Teacher, which is the most important commandment in the law of Moses?" Jesus replied, "'You must love the Lord your God with all your heart, all your soul, and all your mind.' This is the first and greatest commandment."

MATTHEW 22:34-38 NLT

The Pharisees were always trying to trip up Jesus. They wanted nothing more than to find fault with him—a reason to put him on trial or do away with him. When they asked him which of all the commandments was the greatest, they were hoping that he would somehow fail to come up with the correct answer.

Instead, as usual, he got it right. And, oh! How right it was. Isn't it fascinating that the leaders of the day tried to test Jesus? When you get asked difficult questions, you too can rely on God to give you the perfect answers. When you love God fully, you know his heart and priorities become clearer. It's much easier to answer correctly when you speak from the heart.

When we love the Lord our God with all our hearts, everything else falls into place. The other commandments are easy to follow. Have you given all of yourself to God? Do you love the Lord your God with all your heart, all your soul, and all your mind? Let the last of your walls crumble, and give him all of you today.

What do you need to give up
so you can put God first?

God, I know that you desire relationship above everything else. It's hard to say that I love you with everything because I know the truth is that I so often get distracted by other things. But I know that you see my heart, and you know my desire is to love you with my entire being.

O Lord, I have longed for your rescue,
and your instructions are my delight.
Let me live so I can praise you,
and may your regulations help me.
PSALM 119:174-175 NLT

There is wonder to be found in snowflakes, raindrops, and even strange bugs. Though we often don't love the idea of encountering too many of any one of those, if we stop and look, if we allow ourselves to really *see* what is there, it's pretty amazing.

The same can be true of God's Word. It may be displayed in various forms and places throughout our homes, schools, work places, or church buildings, but if we don't stop to really drink in the words that are there, we can miss the rich blessing behind them.

When we believe that God wants to encourage us through his Word, we will no doubt find encouragement in it—because God intended it to be used for that purpose!

Find an encouraging word that you love in the Scriptures today and write it down for daily reflection.

God, help me not to gloss over the beauty and depth of your Word. Only your Word carries the richness of eternity and the encouragement I need for each new day.

Unfailing Goodness

"I am about to go the way of all the earth, and you know in your hearts and souls, all you, that not one thing has failed of all the good things that the Lord your God promised concerning you; all have come to pass for you, not one of them has failed."
JOSHUA 23:14 NRSV

Do you remember the first thing that you failed at? Maybe it was a test at school, a diet, a job interview, or even a relationship. Failure is difficult to admit, especially in a culture that values outward success and appearance. We often hear it said that success comes from many failures, but we only really hear that from successful people!

When Joshua was advanced in years, he reminded the Israelites of all that God had done for them. Though they had been unfaithful to God many times, God remained faithful, and they became a great nation that none could withstand.

God had a plan and a purpose for the nation of Israel, and through his power and mercy he ensured that these plans succeeded. In the same way, God has a purpose for your life, and while you may fail, he will not. Take the opportunity today to submit your heart to his will. Know that not one good thing that God has planned for you will fail.

> *In what ways have you experienced God's faithfulness in your life?*

Thank you, God, for all that you have planned for me. I trust that your plans will not fail. I am humbled by your faithfulness to me. I am sorry that I am not always faithful to you. Help me to submit to your heart and will for my life.

He Is Faithful

Your faithfulness extends to every generation,
as enduring as the earth you created.
PSALM 119:90 NLT

What's the oldest thing you own? How long have
you had it, and what does it mean to you? Whether
a decades-old diamond ring, twenty-year-old car,
or a tattered baby blanket hanging together by
threads, you probably know it won't last forever.
How about your longest relationship? How many
years have you been connected to this person
through the good and the bad? One way we decide
where to place our faith is longevity. History matters.

Consider now what God made: the earth we live
on. Scientists estimate it to be 4.5 billion years old,
give or take fifty million. Whether we think it's been
around that long or six to ten thousand years, it's
some quality workmanship.

If we're looking for someone to trust, we won't find better credentials than that.

Ponder all God has made and all he has done, and share your heart with him regarding his faithfulness. Have you embraced it?

God, through every storm, every disaster, every war, and every attack of the enemy, your creation still stands. Help me to remember who I can depend on… forever.

Ordered Steps

I will instruct you in the way you should go;
I will counsel you with my loving eye on you.
PSALM 32:8 NIV

If you've ever taken the hand of a toddler, you'll know that they are relying on you for their balance. If they stumble, you can easily steady them. This simple act of holding a hand means that you and the child have confidence that they won't fall flat on their face!

In the same way, when we commit our way to God, we are essentially placing our hand in his. He delights in the fact that we are walking with him. Even in the times when we stumble, he will steady our path and give us the confidence to keep walking.

Do you feel like you have stumbled lately, or are unsure of your walk with God? Be confident that the Lord delights in your commitment to him. Accept his hand, continue to walk, and trust him to keep you from falling. As you come to God, ask him to teach you which ways to go. As you spend more time listening to his voice, the way becomes clearer.

In what ways do you find yourself stumbling? How can you draw closer to God to help you in these areas?

Lord, I want to walk into this day holding your hand. Keep a firm grip on me so I don't stumble or fall. I love having you near me. Thank you for sticking close to me. I need more of your guidance in my life, particularly in those areas where I consistently seem to stumble. I ask for your grace to walk more closely in step with your will.

Confident in Incompetence

It is not that we think we are qualified to do anything
on our own. Our qualification comes from God.
2 CORINTHIANS 3:5 NLT

Whether bringing a brand new baby home from
the hospital, giving your first major presentation
at work, or simply making your first meal, there's
probably been at least one moment in your life that
had you thinking, *I have no idea what I'm doing. I'm
not qualified.* So what did you do? Chances are, you
put a smile on your face, dove in, and did your best.

The older we get, the more we realize how truly
helpless we are. We also, beautifully, realize it's okay.

There is great freedom in admitting our shortcomings and allowing the Father to be our strength. No matter what he asks of us, we are confident in our incompetence.

> *What dream or calling would you be able to fulfill if you were to embrace God's competence as your own?*

God, I may not be capable, but you are more than qualified to carry out your plans through me. Help me to swallow my pride and let you lead me.

Approval

*Obviously, I'm not trying to win the approval of people,
but of God. If pleasing people were my goal, I would
not be Christ's servant.*
GALATIANS 1:10 NLT

What motivates you to be spiritual? Do you try to
speak eloquently in church so that other people
will be impressed by what you have to say, or do
you speak out of sincere love for Christ and a desire
to edify his body with truth? Do you raise your
hands in worship so that other people around you
will notice your connection with Christ, or do you
worship because you are so overcome with love for
your Savior?

Our words must be motivated out of love for God, or
they mean nothing. Our praise must be born out of
love for God, or it is just noise. Paul is clear that those
who are trying to please other people are not serving
Christ. Keep your heart and your eyes fixed on God
because he is the only one worthy of your praise.

As you serve Christ and follow him, continually evaluate in your heart whether or not you are acting out of a desire to impress others or God. And remember, you impress God just by being who he created you to be.

> *In what ways do you try to please people?*
> *How can you direct this toward God?*

Jesus, I want to have a genuine heart when I worship you. Help me to turn my attention toward you. I seek to please you only, but I forget that when I am with others. I spend a lot of time trying to please people. Keep me aware of my tendency to seek approval from others. I want my words to be real and to come from a place of loving you.

Hope

May the God of hope fill you with all joy and peace as you trust in him, so that you may overflow with hope by the power of the Holy Spirit.
ROMANS 15:13 NIV

What differentiates hope from a wish? Think about the lottery. Does one hope to win, or wish to win? How about a promotion, a pregnancy, or a proposal? Both hoping and wishing contain desire, but for wishing, that is where it ends.

Hope goes deeper. The strong desire for something good to happen is coupled with a reason to believe that it will.

We see then how vital hope is, and why it's such a beautiful gift. Desire without hope is empty, but together they bring joy, expectancy, and peace. When we put our hope in Christ, he becomes our reason to believe good things will happen. He is our hope.

Allow this blessing from Romans to wash over you today as the Holy Spirit fills you with hope, joy, and peace.

Father, I believe good things will happen in my life. I have wonderful reason to believe this— because my hope in in you, and you are good.

True Religion

Pure and undefiled religion in the sight of our God and Father is this: to visit orphans and widows in their distress, and to keep oneself unstained by the world.
JAMES 1:27 NASB

How can it alleviate their fears, save them from death, and improve their quality of life? Christianity has never been about what we can get from it.

True religion— the kind that is acceptable to God— is found in giving ourselves to those who need the most. It's not about our comfort, our happiness, or even our ticket to heaven. It's about reflecting the glory of Christ on the earth.

The tender Father heart of God is far more interested in developing your love and Christ-like character than he is in keeping you comfortable. His compassion and intense love for mankind will not be satisfied with comfortable, cushioned Christianity.

If you want to bring praise to God, intentionally seek out situations where you can put into practice your undefiled religion.

God, I want to make it my mission to meet needs, to love, and to bring life. I know you want this too, and I can't do it without you. Give me your love for others so I have plenty to draw from.

Humility

Humility is the fear of the LORD;
its wages are riches and honor and life
PROVERBS 22:4 NIV

God values humility over pride and earthly success. That is why sometimes God makes us wait before revealing his plans for us. In the waiting is where he grows us in humility. When things don't work out perfectly, our pride is dismantled and we learn the most valuable lessons.

God being glorified in our lives doesn't make sense to our humanity because his plan isn't our plan and his ways are different. The entire message of the Gospel is upside-down from what we know here on earth. In God's kingdom, humility is elevated and pride is made low. Those who are poor are rich, and those who are weak are strong.

God is more concerned with having your heart fully devoted to him than he is with you having a successful ministry.

Humble yourself in God's presence today.

God, I know you want me to serve you and you love when I prosper in kingdom work, but these are not your main goal. You really just want to be with me forever. I am so blessed and humbled by that.

Give Me Liberty

*Now you are free from the power of sin and have
become slaves of God. Now you do those things that
lead to holiness and result in eternal life.*
ROMANS 6:22 NLT

Freedom is a place without obligations. Freedom is
to live exempt from debts, constraints, and bonds.
Our obligation for the sins we've committed is to
satisfy justice. Our souls cannot be free without
a release from our debt of sin, and the currency
demanded for a soul is death.

When our debt was paid by the death of Jesus, the
truest form of freedom was declared over our soul.
Our chains were broken, and our liberty was granted.
When Jesus returned to heaven, he left his Spirit
with us because where his Spirit is, there is freedom.

There is a freedom waiting for you that will challenge any preconceived notions you've had of freedom. There is liberty in the presence of the Spirit of God that is unprecedented. God wants you to walk forward out of sin and into the life of freedom that he intended for you. Leave your obligation at his feet—it's taken care of.

What is your biggest challenge to freedom? Ask God for his strength to overcome this.

Jesus, you have paid my debt and I am therefore no longer in darkness. Help me to be faithful in my freedom and to show others your love so that they can be set free too. I am no longer bound by sin. Let your light shine brightly from my life today.

Redeemed and Free

The Spirit of the Lord is upon me,
because he has anointed me
to proclaim good news to the poor.
He has sent me to proclaim liberty to the captives
and recovering of sight to the blind,
to set at liberty those who are oppressed,
to proclaim the year of the Lord's favor.
ISAIAH 61:1-2 ESV

When Jesus, the long-awaited Messiah, revealed his deity to his family, his disciples, and the crowds, they were expecting a mighty king who would deliver them from their oppressors and establish his everlasting kingdom.

What they got was a humble servant who dined with tax collectors and whose feet were cleansed by the tears of a prostitute. Jesus wasn't exactly what they thought he would be.

He was better! He came to bring salvation to those who were drowning in a sea of sin and sickness; those who were cast out and in need of holy redemption; those whom the religious leaders had deemed unworthy but whose hearts longed for true restoration. He came to redeem his people, but not in the way they expected.

> *How do you think people's expectations of the Messiah made it difficult to accept him when he came?*

Jesus, you delivered me from the bonds of sin and oppression through your death and resurrection. I praise you for my freedom! Holy Spirit, rest upon me and give me boldness to speak to others about this good news.

Hidden Beauty

*Let your adorning be the hidden person of the heart
with the imperishable beauty of a gentle and quiet
spirit, which in God's sight is very precious.*
1 PETER 3:4 ESV

Beauty is a powerful influencer in the lives of
women. We are constantly bombarded with images
and messages of what beauty is and what it should
be. Even if we are confident in who we are, it can
still be difficult not to give in to the subtle thoughts
of not being good enough. The awful truth about
outward beauty is that no matter how much time,
attention, and investment you put into it, beauty can
never really last. Our appearance inevitably changes
over time, and our physical beauty does fade.

In a world where we are constantly told to beautify
ourselves so we will be noticed, the concept of
adorning the hidden person of the heart sounds
almost make-believe. But what it comes down to
is the truth that the most important opinion we
should seek is the opinion of our Creator.

It might sound trite or cliché, but when we step away from the distraction of the media circus and all the lies it has told us, the truth becomes clear. Your gentle and quiet spirit is precious to God. You were made to delight the heart of God. Nothing delights him more than your heart, turned toward your Savior and clothed in the imperishable beauty of a peaceful spirit flowing with gentleness, kindness, and goodness.

> *How can you see gentleness and a quiet spirit affect your day-to-day life?*

Heavenly Father, as I hurriedly get dressed for the day, help me to remember that my inward beauty is more important than the outward. I don't always feel beautiful, even on the inside. I choose to dwell on the fact that you have made me beautiful. Help me to carry a gentle and quiet spirit into a busy world.

The Father's Love

*"If a man has a hundred sheep but one of the sheep
gets lost, he will leave the other ninety-nine on the hill
and go to look for the lost sheep. I tell you the truth,
if he finds it he is happier about that one sheep than
about the ninety-nine that were never lost."*
MATTHEW 18:12-13 NCV

Regardless of how beautifully or how imperfectly
your earthly father showed his love, your heavenly
Father's love is utterly boundless. Rest in that
thought a moment. There is nothing you can do to
change how he feels about you. Nothing.

We spend so much time trying to make ourselves
more lovable, from beauty regimens to gourmet
baking, to being there for pretty much everyone.

It's easy to forget we are already perfectly loved. Our Father loves us more than we can imagine. And he would do anything for us. Anything.

Who do you love most fiercely, most protectively, most desperately here on earth? What would you do for them? Know that it's a mere fraction, nearly immeasurable, of what God would do for you.

God, I thank you for your complete and astounding love for me. You come search me out when I am lost and you rejoice when you find me. Thank you for watching over me.

The Real Thing

When they arrived, Samuel took one look at Eliab and thought, "Surely this is the LORD's anointed!"
But the LORD said to Samuel, "Don't judge by his appearance or height, for I have rejected him. The LORD doesn't see things the way you see them. People judge by outward appearance, but the Lord looks at the heart."
1 SAMUEL 16:6-7 NLT

Is that real? Whether jewelry, hair color, purse, or body part, there's real, and there's imitation. Neither choice is inherently wrong or right. Why we choose as we do—and where we compromise—reveals our hearts. And it's our hearts that matter to God.

Make no mistake, a sister who shuns makeup and hasn't painted her house trim in years can be every bit as guilty of vanity and pride as one who won't leave her own bedroom until she appears flawless and has an eight-person grounds crew.

When we spend a moment checking our internal beauty, we're sometimes sorely disappointed at what we find. God isn't finished with us yet! If we let him, he will continue to make us more beautiful on the inside—where it really counts.

> *Spend some time examining your heart with God today.*

God, you don't care how much I spend on shoes, how much time I spend in front of the mirror, or how fabulous my home is. But you do care about why those things matter—or don't—to me. Help me to want the right things for the right reasons.

Flip the Switch

The way of the good person is like the light of dawn,
growing brighter and brighter until full daylight.
But the wicked walk around in the dark;
they can't even see what makes them stumble.
PROVERBS 4:18-19 NCV

Have you ever walked through your home at night, thinking that you could make it without turning a light on, only to stumble on something unexpectedly set in your path?

When you cannot see where you are going, you are likely to get tripped up. On the other hand, your way is obvious when you simply turn on a light.

The Bible tells us that walking in righteousness is just like walking in the bright light of day. But choosing rebellion is like stumbling around in a deep darkness. You never know what hit you until it's already too late.

Are you choosing the light? Is your path brightly lit? Or are you standing in total darkness? If so, then flip the switch! Pray that you will make wise choices.

God, I seek your wisdom for my life. You shine brightly for me. I let you in today and ask that you will be my eternal light, illuminating my days.

The Plan

It was by faith that Abraham obeyed when God called him to leave home and go to another land that God would give him as his inheritance. He went without knowing where he was going.
HEBREWS 11:8 NLT

We all like to have a map laid out for us to see every bend and every turn in the road. As Christians, we spend so much of our time searching for the "will of God." Often when it comes to the will of God, we can, quite honestly, just miss the point. We look for what God wants us to do, but we miss out on seeing who he is. God knows what he is doing. Most of the time he won't tell you what he will do, he will just show you who he is.

We aren't always going to know where we're headed. But the heart of God is for us to know him. Not to know every detail of the plan. Not to know what someone else's story is. Just to know him for who he is.

When you abide in Jesus, only then can he truly accomplish his perfect will in you. Come before him and strip away your questions and your need to know the plan. Just come before him needing to know only him. He will not withhold himself from you.

> *What is God encouraging you to trust him with now?*

Father, I'm not sure where I am going today, or what I am going to do. Lead me today, and every day, and help me to have faith that you are guiding me into what is best for my life. Be present with me right now. Guide me, guard me, and show me the light of truth. Give me courage to trust the way that you are leading me.

"If you try to hang on to your life, you will lose it. But if you give up your life for my sake, you will save it."
MATTHEW 16:25 NLT

The key to growing in your faith is simple. There must be less of us in order to have more of God. To allow more of his presence into our lives, we must give up more of ourselves. We need to place our lives before him as an offering and give him our all.

The world would say that giving up ourselves is a loss. We've been taught for years that we must put ourselves first. Our fellow man would say that we need to make ourselves a priority. But oh, are they missing out!

When we give ourselves over completely to God, we get to share in his glory and in his great joy. Setting aside our earthly pleasures for heavenly treasures means we gain a lot more than what this world could ever offer us.

Empty yourself of the desires of your flesh and allow God to fill you with his presence.

God, as I empty myself of selfish desires, I won't feel a lack. Thank you that it will cause me to overflow with life and light, spilling out everywhere for others to see. I know that I need to become less so I can gain more of you.

Eternal Perspective

God has made everything beautiful for its own time.
He has planted eternity in the human heart, but even
so, people cannot see the whole scope of God's work
from beginning to end.
ECCLESIASTES 3:11 NLT

Much emphasis is placed on figuring life out. We so easily become caught up in the here-and-now that we lose sight of the fact that life on earth is really only a blink compared to what our life will be in eternity.

Our entire agendas will shift when we begin to live with eternal perspective. Once we understand that the only things that will last are those of spiritual worth, we suddenly realize that our priorities must be adjusted. Our eternal worth must supersede our earthly value. We can be among the world's most wealthy here but be headed for eternal destruction. Or we could be living paycheck to paycheck in this life and be governor of half a kingdom in the next.

You have the unique opportunity to determine how you will spend your forever life. Serve God well with your one short life on earth, so that you can live endlessly with him in glory.

> *How is what you are doing right now preparing you for eternity?*

I want to serve you well today, God. I get caught up in all the distractions of this life but I know that eternity sits in my heart. Help me to uncover your eternal workings in my life today. Reveal something of long lasting worth to me. Thank you that you have started to make me beautiful and you will continue to make me beautiful right into eternity. I don't know what you are doing from beginning to end, but I trust that you know all things.

In Sunshine and Storm

When times are good, be happy;
but when times are bad, consider this:
God has made the one as well as the other.
Therefore, no one can discover
anything about their future.
ECCLESIASTES 7:14 NIV

It's easy to feel happy on a sunny day, when all is well, the birds are singing, and life is going along swimmingly. But what happens when waters are rougher, bad news comes, or the days feel just plain hard?

God wants us to feel gladness when times are good. He has made each and every day. We are called to rejoice in all of them whether good or bad. Happiness is determined by our circumstances, but true joy comes when we can find the silver linings, hidden in our darkest hours—when we can sing his praises no matter what.

We don't know what the future holds for us here on earth, but we can find our delight in the knowledge that our eternity is set in beauty.

Is your happiness determined by your circumstance? Pray that you will discover true joy in our Creator.

God, give me a deep and abiding satisfaction in each day that goes beyond my human understanding. Help me to see the beauty in the future you have for me.

Bold and Confident

My voice You shall hear in the morning, O Lord;
In the morning I will direct it to You,
And I will look up.
PSALM 5:3 NKJV

Each and every day, we are given the most incredible opportunity. We are given the chance to talk to a God who has been in our shoes. A man who literally walked the walk. He is waiting for us to walk up to him and ask him anything.

Jesus went through the same things we do during his time on earth, so he truly understands where we're coming from when we approach him. We don't need to muster up our courage! He wants us to be confident.

Esther was bold when she approached her king about saving her people, and that guy was known to make rash and terrible decisions! We get to talk to a King who is known for his mercy.

Are you holding back tentatively in your time with your heavenly King? Be bold, and be confident!

Father, thank you that you love me. You understand me. You want what's best for me. I am so grateful that you show me grace and mercy wherever and whenever I seek it from you.

Dance Unhindered

"It was before the LORD, who chose me rather than your father or anyone from his house when he appointed me ruler over the LORD's people Israel—I will celebrate before the LORD. I will become even more undignified than this, and I will be humiliated in my own eyes. But by these slave girls you spoke of, I will be held in honor."
2 SAMUEL 6:21-22 NIV

Peer pressure is real, even for adults. We often worry about how we will look in the eyes of others. *Do I look okay today?* we wonder. *I forgot to bring the garbage can in. What will the neighbors think?* we ask ourselves.

There was at least one person who didn't care what others thought of him. King David was so excited after winning a big battle that he went whooping and dancing, praising God as he marched home to his family. When his wife scorned him for looking foolish, he had no time for her words.

When others look down on you for being who you are, just let it go. Dance before God without a care of what others think. He loves when you honor him by letting go of your pride.

Are you worried about what others think, or are you concerned with what God thinks of you?

God, today I dance in your presence. I don't care what it looks like! I want to celebrate life with you and I know you delight in rejoicing with me too.

Chosen and Called

Moses said to the Lord, "Please, Lord, I have never been a skilled speaker. Even now, after talking to you, I cannot speak well. I speak slowly and can't find the best words."
EXODUS 4:10 NCV

When God asks us to do something, our first instinct is often to look around at who we feel could do it better. We wonder why God didn't choose that person, who—in our eyes—is clearly more qualified than we are.

God could have chosen anyone to be his mouthpiece and his leader for the incredible work he did with the Israelites. He picked Moses. He knew what Moses' strengths and weaknesses were before he called him. And he still picked Moses.

Do you ever feel like God shouldn't have picked you for something? Do you think it would have been smarter for him to pick someone who is more creative, more intelligent, or more eloquent? You may not understand why God picked you for a certain task, but you can trust that when he calls you to do something, it's because he knows that you are not only capable, you are the one he wants to do the job.

What are you doing right now that you see God has called you to? What is he calling you further into?

God, I don't want to question you when you call me. I don't often feel qualified enough to do what you want me to do, and yet I can't ignore the call that you have on my life. You didn't give this to anyone else, you gave it to me. Give me confidence to continue in the good works that you have given me to do.

Eye on You

In him we were also chosen, having been predestined according to the plan of him who works out everything in conformity with the purpose of his will, in order that we, who were the first to put our hope in Christ, might be for the praise of his glory.
EPHESIANS 1:11-12 NIV

Did you know that long before you decided to take the plunge and accept Christ into your heart as your Savior, he had his eye on you? He was waiting for you to come to him so that he could share with you his eternal gift.

God wanted glorious living for you. And oh, how he celebrated when you made that decision!

It is through Christ that we discover who we are. When we put our hope in him, we find ourselves. It's in him that we learn what we are living for. And he works all of our lives together as Christians for the greater good.

You were chosen by God. He waited for you, and he rejoiced when you came to him. Celebrate with him today!

I praise you, God, for the gift you have given me in eternal salvation. You are so good!

Sustained

I lie down and sleep;
I wake again, for the Lord sustains me.
PSALM 3:5 NRSV

There is always something to worry about, isn't there? Whether it's health, finances, relationships, or details, there are many unknowns in life that can easily keep us worrying. But what if we stopped worrying? What if we stopped questioning and decided instead to feel peace? What if we could trust completely that God would take care of us and our loved ones. God is our rock and he alone will sustain us.

There will be many unknowns in your life. There will be moments when the rug feels as though it's been pulled out from under you, and there is nothing to do but despair. In those moments that you can't control, you can trust. You can rest your soul, your mind, and your body in the hands of the one who has the power to sustain you.

The words in Psalm 3 can bring us comfort and peace when we are fearful. It speaks volumes about the grace of God: the protection and safety of his hand. But the verse goes beyond peace and comfort to the power of God. When we trust and believe in this God who possesses the power of life and death, what do we have to fear? Our entire lives are in his hands. We can't change that fact, so we might as well rest in it.

What is interfering with your ability to rest? Ask God to give you a solution so you can rest physically and spiritually.

God, today I face the unknown. Let me rest in the knowledge that you will sustain me. I need that rest. I need to rest my body, and I need to rest my soul. I believe you have the power of life and death, so I ask that you will continue to sustain me.

Thirst for Pure Water

*I want more than anything
to be in the courtyards of the LORD's Temple.
My whole being wants
to be with the living God.*
PSALM 84:2 NCV

Have you ever noticed that the more consistently you drink water, the more your body thirsts for it? And the less you drink water, the less you consciously desire it. Though you still need water to live, you become satisfied with small amounts of it disguised in other foods and drinks. But for a body that has become accustomed to pure water on a daily basis, only straight water will quench its thirst.

The same principle applies to God's presence in our lives. The more we enter his presence, the more we long to stay there. The more we sit at his feet and listen to what he has to say, the more we need his Word to continue living.

If we allow ourselves to become satisfied with candy-coated truth and second hand revelation, we will slowly begin to lose our hunger for the pure, untainted presence of the living God.

Does your entire being long to be with God? Press into Jesus until you no longer can be satisfied with anything less than the purest form of his presence.

Cultivate my hunger and fascination with you, God, until I literally crave you. I want to spend my life feasting on your truth, knowing your character, and adoring your heart.

Stumbling in the Dark

The Word gave life to everything that was created,
and his life brought light to everyone.
The light shines in the darkness,
and the darkness can never extinguish it.
JOHN 1:4-5 NLT

Have you ever walked somewhere in the pitch black? You bump into things, knock stuff over, and often can't even place where you are or where you're going. Everything becomes muddled in the darkness. Without light to guide us, we can't see where we're going, or what we're running into.

Many times throughout the Bible, God likens being in sin to being in darkness. When we immerse ourselves in sin, thus rejecting the light of the truth, we can no longer see what we are running into. By allowing sinful messages to enter our souls through different avenues, we lose our ability to navigate our lives.

When wickedness begins to overtake your life, you lose the ability to recognize what is making you sin. Strive to keep your soul sensitive to the truth. Keep sight of the light by spending time in God's Word.

Who can you share the light of Christ with this week?

God, shine your light into my heart. Illuminate my sin so that I can repent and be free of the darkness. I want to walk without stumbling today. Thank you that darkness cannot stand up to light. Now that I know the truth of your ways, the darkness has been expelled and my faith in you will never be extinguished. Help me to shine the light into other people around me so they will be exposed to your truth.

Perfection

His divine power has granted to us everything
pertaining to life and godliness, through the true
knowledge of Him who called us by His own glory
and excellence.
2 PETER 1:3 NASB

Each of us is keenly aware of our own weaknesses. We know all our flaws too well and we make eliminating them our goal. But no matter how much effort we put out, we can never and will never achieve perfection.

Despite most of us realizing that we will never be perfect, we still put unreasonable pressure on ourselves. Whether in a task, in our character, or in our walk with Christ, we easily become frustrated when we reach for perfection and can't grasp it.

If we allow perfectionism to drive our performance, then we will quench our own potential and inhibit our effectiveness. Let the pressure of being perfect be washed away in God's mercy.

> *When you mess up, God has to take over and the result of that action is always perfection.*

God, thank you for the freedom to not be perfect. Your power is all the more perfect when displayed in my weakness. When I am not the main point, you are. That's the way it should be.

Our Advocate

My little children, I am writing these things to you so that you may not sin. But if anyone does sin, we have an advocate with the Father, Jesus Christ the righteous.
1 JOHN 2:1 ESV

It says in Isaiah that no matter which way we go, we will hear a voice saying, "This is the way, walk in it." But it is often so hard to hear that voice—and harder still to distinguish it from the other voices in our lives.

You have a mediator between yourself and the almighty God. It is someone who loved you enough to lay down everything for you. Surely a man who loves you with that kind of intensity also loves you enough to forgive your imperfections?

We stumble and fall every single day. We hear wrong, and we miss the mark continuously. We fall into sin when all we were chasing after was righteousness, and we feel guilt even when we know we've been given grace. Rest in the fact that God is gracious, that he knows your humanity and he compensates for it.

> *How do you need to experience God's help in your life right now?*

Thank you, Jesus, for helping me to overcome my sin. Thank you for showing me that there is a way out of sin, and that there is a better way. I am forgiven. Thank you for making me whole again, and for cleansing me from thoughts and actions that are not compatible with your kingdom.

Victory

*Thank God! He gives us victory over sin and death
through our Lord Jesus Christ.
So, my dear brothers and sisters,
be strong and immovable.*
1 CORINTHIANS 15:57-58 NLT

Have you ever watched one of those movie battle scenes where the good guys are grossly outnumbered? You wince as the evil army swoops in with thousands of troops carrying sophisticated weapons. While the good army has a lot of heart, you know they don't stand much of a chance. But when it all seems lost, out of nowhere, reinforcements arrive in a surge of hope. Suddenly, they go from losing terribly to winning victoriously!

Daily, we are engaged in our own battle against sin. Left to ourselves, we don't have the strength necessary to win the fight. But when it seems all hope is lost, our reinforcement—Jesus Christ— arrives, and we gain the strength to boldly obtain the victory over sin.

You may go through seasons in your life when you feel like sin has you outnumbered. Temptation is great, and you don't feel that you have the strength to overcome it. But know that you don't have to fight alone. You have the power of God on your side, and he has already won against sin and death. Embrace victory over sin as you thank Jesus for his work on the cross.

Where do you need to see the victorious Christ reign in your life again?

Jesus, forgive my sins and help me to gain the victory over any darkness that would try to creep back into my life. I feel like I am confessing sin to you time and time again, yet I know you want me to recognize that I already have the victory. You won this victory on the cross and I no longer have to live in guilt and shame because you have set me free!

Stillness

Be still, and know that I am God;
I will be exalted among the nations,
I will be exalted in the earth!
PSALM 46:10 NKJV

Dusk settles on a chilly winter night. A gray fog hovers and snow begins to fall: cold, blustering snow…the kind that sticks. The snow keeps coming until you can barely see one hundred feet in front of you. In the woods it's quiet; all you can hear is the gentle wind, and all you can see is snow and trees. A pure white blanket of snow restores the earth, and as it falls, it restores you.

Sometimes we have to get outside of the noise and chaos of our own four walls. We have to step out into the snow, or the sun, or the breeze. We have to get alone, get silent, and clear the clutter from our minds and hearts as we stand in God's natural sanctuary.

There is so much power in the stillness of knowing God as you stand serene in the world he created.

The busyness of your life will always be there, but never forget to take the moments you can, to stop and know your God.

In these precious moments I spend with you, God, I find refreshment and strength to take on whatever will come next.

Our Father in Heaven

The eyes of the L ORD watch over those who do right;
his ears are open to their cries for help.
P SALM 34:15 NLT

Do we know in the depths of our hearts that our prayers are heard: both the shouting cries for help and the gentle whispers of thanksgiving? He knows our every thought before we even think it. This is the Father that created us and calls us by name. We are his beloved children.

Believe it. We need to let the truth sink into the very deepest parts of our hearts and rest there in thanksgiving. His Word is truth, and he tells us time and time again that he will answer our prayer because we trust in him (see 1 Chronicles 5:20).

Whether through song, action, thought, or speech, God delights in hearing our prayers.

Do you take time daily to pray to your loving Father? If not, start the practice of talking with him in the car, in the shower, or sitting in silence in your room.

Thank you, God, that what I say to you doesn't have to be fancy or long. You desire my honest conversation and communion with you more than a thousand pretty words.

"I have this against you, that you have abandoned the love you had at first."
REVELATION 2:4 ESV

"How did the two of you meet?" We ask the inevitable question, starry-eyed, knowing the romance and dreamy memories that will tumble out. Every love story has a beginning—a first look, a first word, a first thought—the creation of love itself.

What does the beginning of your love story with God look like? Was there a song that you can remember falling in love with him to? Maybe there was a verse—a word from his very mouth that captured your heart. Or is there something about the place you were in when your heart responded to his and you walked away changed? It's all too easy to lose the initial passion of love. God becomes woven into our lives like a single thread in a tapestry.

Search your heart today. Have you abandoned the depth of love you had at first? Have you strayed from that place where all you wanted was him and all you needed was his presence? Take some time to remember everything about the moment in which you fell in love with God. Sometimes we have to remember how we fell in love to remind ourselves that we are in love.

What will help you remember your love for God in the days to come?

Jesus, I remember what it was like when I first knew that I was loved by you. I felt so passionate about you! Return that passion to me, even in the middle of a busy day; let my gaze rest on you. You have been so good to me. I know that you remain faithful, even when I forget to acknowledge that you are the source of my life. Return me to that place of loving you with all that I am.

Mystery and Hope

Since through God's mercy we have this ministry, we do not lose heart. Rather, we have renounced secret and shameful ways; we do not use deception, nor do we distort the word of God. On the contrary, by setting forth the truth plainly we commend ourselves to everyone's conscience in the sight of God…For God, who said, "Let light shine out of darkness," made his light shine in our hearts to give us the light of the knowledge of God's glory displayed in the face of Christ.

2 CORINTHIANS 4:1-2, 6 NIV

There is much mystery in life. So many unanswered questions and unknowns. Faith in and of itself is a huge element of mystery. In order to live a faith-filled life, we accept the elements of mystery because we know what goes hand-in-hand with it…hope.

Hope is God telling us that his purpose is bigger than any unknown. When we walk through anything, no matter how great a mystery, God is walking alongside us.

God doesn't promise us an explanation, and therein lies the mystery. But he does promise his presence, and that is an unfailing truth. When we walk through deep waters, he is there.

> *Have you had a moment of mystery? An unexplained circumstance or situation that you wish you could ask God about?*

Father, I know deep in my heart that hope is waiting on the other end of the mystery.

Gratitude

Whatever you do, whether in word or deed, do it all in the name of the Lord Jesus, giving thanks to God the Father through him.
COLOSSIANS 3:17 NIV

Have you ever noticed on vacation that your heart feels lighter? That you worry less and are more thankful? Cultivating a heart of thankfulness can shift our entire perspective on life. When we are grateful, we start to see the light of God more. We start to see him everywhere.

A thankful heart is a heart that refuses to let the enemy in and deceive us. Suddenly, our circumstances seem not so terrible, our problems not so huge. A heart of gratitude glorifies God and keeps us centered on him.

Allow Christ into your heart today, even though it will be full of things to do, people to see, jobs to take care of. Be thankful as you do the day-to-day things and cultivate that heart for giving thanks! A heart of thankfulness keeps you grounded in Christ and allows you to live the fullest life he's designed for you.

What can you do to start cultivating a heart of gratitude?

God, be so present in my life today that I can't help but think about you and all the wonderful people and things you have placed in my life. Help me to be thankful even in times of trial. Thank you for the ups that make me smile and the downs that build resilience. Thank you for the good and the bad. Help me to be thankful in everything.

Gems

The heartfelt counsel of a friend
is as sweet as perfume and incense.
PROVERBS 27:9 NLT

When you sign up for a competitive team sport, you have a basic understanding that you're going to have to work hard and that emotions will run high to win and succeed. You know that you'll win some, you'll lose some, and that somewhere along the way you'll start to feel good about playing the game whether you win or lose.

Playing a competitive team sport can sometimes feel the same as building relationships with other women. We win some—forming incredible relationships—and others we lose. We were created uniquely, and while we are asked to love one another, it doesn't mean that we hope for a best-friend relationship with each woman we meet.

When we do find those friends, those precious few who make us better people by encouraging us and making us laugh, we need to hold on tight and enjoy the rare gems they are.

Do you have a friend that holds you accountable but also lifts you up when you need it? Share how much that friend means to you today.

God, I thank you for friends that hold me accountable. I ask that you would continue to bring people into my life that challenge me and encourage me in my walk with you.

Since, then, you have been raised with Christ, set your hearts on things above, where Christ is, seated at the right hand of God. Set your minds on things above, not on earthly things.
COLOSSIANS 3:1-2 NIV

Social media: an escape, a gift, a communicative tool, a joy stealer, a comparison thief, a comedian, entertainment. Social media can be fun. But it can also become an idol when we don't recognize it as such. Suddenly, instead of opening up the Bible, we are clicking on our phones checking Facebook, posting photos, and updating statuses seeking attention and approval from people rather than our Creator.

God's desire for our life is that we chose him above all else. He wants to be our focal point, one we return to time and again, so we don't ever steer too far off course. Instead of seeking approval from others, we turn our eyes toward the one who loves us most, whose voice is the only one we should hear.

In a busy life of choices, it's important to know your back-up is also your best option—seeking God and choosing life with him.

Where do you choose to spend the majority of your time? What choices could you eliminate to stay centered on Jesus?

Jesus, I choose to listen to your voice, right now. Still my heart, calm my mind, and speak because I am listening. Help me to dwell on what is better. I get wrapped up in menial things and I waste time. Give me strength to switch my thoughts from worthless things to you in all your beauty and goodness.

Love Well

Follow God's example, therefore, as dearly loved children and walk in the way of love, just as Christ loved us and gave himself up for us as a fragrant offering and sacrifice to God.
EPHESIANS 5:1-2 NIV

If we do anything right, let it be that we love well. Loving well looks different for each person, but we know it when we do it: when we love whole-heartedly. We can't change the entire world—only Jesus can do that—but we can change the world for one person.

There are big things you can do to love well, but loving well can be done in little, everyday moments too.

We love despite feelings. We love when it's tough. We love when we don't necessarily want to. We love well because we are called to: because God loved us first.

In what ways can you love well?
Are there some you don't feel you love well
that you can aim higher for?

God, help me love the way you do. Please give me your heart for those you have placed in my life. I cannot love in my own strength.

The Voice of Love

"The Father gives me the people who are mine.
Every one of them will come to me,
and I will always accept them."
JOHN 6:37 NCV

When we live for other voices, we will quickly become worn out and discouraged. Other people's expectations for how we should live, act, and be are sometimes unreachable. There is only one voice that matters, and it can come in a variety of forms—the voice of God.

Nothing you do or don't do is going to make God love you any more or any less. Soak it in, so you can drown out all the other voices. God tells us that we are loved, we are cherished, and we have significant value. We are his beloved, his children, his beautiful creation. This is the voice that matters.

God's voice is the one to come back to when you feel like you're not enough. He will encourage you and remind you that you are.

What are the voices you typically listen to? Can you ignore them and focus only on the voice that matters?

Father, I know there will be a lot of voices in my day. Help me to listen to the ones that matter, and most importantly to listen to yours. Thank you for being the one true voice in my life. Help me to recognize when I am dwelling on the wrong voices and conversations, and bring me back to your Word.

The Call for Help

I look up to the hills,
but where does my help come from?
My help comes from the LORD,
who made heaven and earth
PSALM 121:1-2 NCV

Depending on the type of person you are, you may not be very good at asking for help. There are those who like to be the helpers: they do best serving others because they feel capable and useful. Then there are those who gladly accept service any time they are given the opportunity. Neither is better than the other, and both have their positive elements.

In different seasons of life, natural helpers may need to be the ones receiving help. Sometimes this is hard to accept, and we have to be careful not to let pride take control.

Asking for help is part of being vulnerable: we push everything aside to say, "I can't do this alone." God has put people in our lives who love to help, but they won't know we need it until we ask.

Can you easily ask for help? God asks you to take a chance on the people he's intricately placed in your life.

Thank you, God, for the people you have placed in my life for me to lean on. I am amazed by how much stronger I feel when I have someone to help me carry the load. I want to be that person for others as well.

Break Every Chain

"His purpose in all this is that they should seek after God, and perhaps feel their way toward him and find him—though he is not far from any one of us."
ACTS 17:27 TLB

There is a chance to start over—every day if we need to. From the inside out, we can be transformed and our hearts renewed. We can essentially remake ourselves with the help, healing, and transformative nature of Christ.

Jesus died on the cross to promise us a life free from the bondage of sin, free from hopelessness, free from any chains that try to trap us. In Christ, we are set free. We need to hear the truth of Christ's promise for us and stop the cycle of hopelessness, defeat, and bondage to sin. All we need to do is get on our knees and pray.

Wait for God's voice to permeate the deepest, saddest parts of you. He wants you to let him take care of you. He is pursuing your heart.

Is there an area of your life that you need to receive freedom from?

God, I want to start this day new. I seek to follow your heart in everything that I do today, and I thank you that you will not be far from me. When I am tired, and feeling a little defeated, I choose to give those feelings to you and ask that you draw near to me.

Cheer for the Prize

May the God who gives endurance and encouragement give you the same attitude of mind toward each other that Christ Jesus had.
ROMANS 15:5 NIV

Have you ever watched cheerleaders at a sporting event? Smiling, bubbly, energetic, yelling for their beloved team. What we don't see is what might be going on underneath all of that encouragement. Everyone has their issues. And yet there they are, faithfully devoted to their team because they know the prize at the end.

In this same way, let us encourage one another in our faith. Imagine our Abba Father's joy when he sees us lifting each other up in praise and loving despite whatever we might have going on.

There is so much to be gained in relationship with other believers whether on the receiving or giving end. And the prize at the end is eternity. There is nothing greater.

What are some ways you can encourage others?

God, I know you delight in seeing me give of my time and talents. You have blessed me with talents for the specific purpose of sharing with others. Help me not to be selfish with my gifts.

In the Secret

"When you pray, do not be like the hypocrites, for they love to pray standing in the synagogues and on the street corners to be seen by others. Truly I tell you, they have received their reward in full. But when you pray, go into your room, close the door and pray to your Father, who is unseen. Then your Father, who sees what is done in secret, will reward you."
MATTHEW 6:5-6 NIV

Cherish the secret things. So much of our life is for others. So much. Whether it is the requirement of jobs, keeping up relationships, or the programs we volunteer for, a lot of our time and energy is spent on other people.

God wants our time. He wants it for us and for him. Maybe this will require a designated prayer closet, or a quiet place away. Find it today.

Head to a quiet place with your Bible as soon as you get a chance. You might have to read this with noise all around you. What's important is that you dedicate your time to God. However you get your time, your heavenly Father sees you. What a faithful gift that thought is; he sees you in secret and will meet you where you are.

Can you get away today in secret to pray?
In secret, God will reward your heart.
Make sneaking away with him a daily routine.

God, I pray that I don't become religious with the way that I spend time with you. I want to engage with you at any moment of any day, and I don't need it to be loud and pretentious. Let me be genuine in my prayers to you. Thank you that we don't have to make a fuss about this time, but it's something that we can both enjoy.

Cycle

To the praise of the glory of His grace, which He freely bestowed on us in the Beloved. In Him we have redemption through His blood, the forgiveness of our trespasses, according to the riches of His grace which He lavished on us.
EPHESIANS 1:6-8 NASB

Have you ever said or done something that you immediately regretted? It just happened: that horrible moment that we replay over and over again. Then, maybe a few days later, something similar happens. Why does this happen? Why can't we exercise more self-control?

Those moments are the vicious cycle of our humanness. Thankfully, through the blood of Jesus Christ and our repentance, we are forgiven, set free, and released of the burden of our mistakes. We are given a clean slate to start over. And some days that gift feels bigger than others.

Some days we rely heavily on the grace of our Lord and Savior just to get through the day. And that is okay.

Have you had a "moment" recently? Do you know you are forgiven through the blood of Jesus?

God, I accept your gift; I am forgiven. Help me to forgive myself and keep moving forward.

Fill the Gap

"Blessed are the poor in spirit,
for theirs is the kingdom of heaven.
Blessed are those who mourn,
for they will be comforted.
Blessed are the meek,
for they will inherit the earth.
Blessed are those who hunger and thirst for
righteousness,
for they will be filled."
MATTHEW 5:3-6 NIV

There are days where you might wake up a little more sluggish, with a little less energy and positivity about the day. That can feel kind of empty, a gap you're hoping to fill.

The great thing about the God you serve is that in him, you can be complete. He can be that gap-filler. As you sit with him, his light begins to burn brighter. Meet God in dependence. Present your helplessness and emptiness to him and he will bless you and fill your gap with warmth, joy, peace, care, and love.

As you spend time with God, allow him to speak to you and rest knowing you can be transformed and filled even on the hardest days. He is faithful and loving no matter your circumstance or feeling.

Have you seen the fruit of this promise on one of your rough days?

Father, lift me up today. It's hard to get out of bed, and sometimes I feel anxious or worried about the day ahead. Give me energy and strength to face another day. I'm glad to be here in your presence. It is a struggle for me to just sit down and think about you when my mind is so full of other things. As I seek you, let the things of this earth grow dim in the light of your glory.

We are surrounded by a great cloud of people whose lives tell us what faith means. So let us run the race that is before us and never give up. We should remove from our lives anything that would get in the way and the sin that so easily holds us back. Let us look only to Jesus, the One who began our faith and who makes it perfect. He suffered death on the cross. But he accepted the shame as if it were nothing because of the joy that God put before him. And now he is sitting at the right side of God's throne.

HEBREWS 12:1-2 NCV

God provides us relief from any bondage we carry. He truly does. Our Father can take any mistake we've made in the past and release the beauty in that error. We don't need to be so hard on ourselves. We don't need to feel trapped, or think we've failed, or hold on so tightly that we can't see the joy in our current circumstance.

Have you been stressed about being trapped in sin or burdened by worry? Turn your face toward God and let him break your bondage apart. He can take the journey and form it into a place of humility and empathy for others.

Watch as the chains break and you walk away much, much lighter.

> *What are the mistakes you've made in the past that you have trouble letting go of? Take a few minutes to let God's promise of redemption make way into your heart. And then forgive yourself.*

Jesus, thank you for your forgiveness. Thank you that you keep cheering me on even when I stumble. Be gracious to me today, so I can persevere in all that you have laid before me. Help me to have the end destination in mind. Please let me see beyond the wrong things I have done, as you do. Help me to know that you are creating a positive witness out of my walk with you.

Highways

"My thoughts are not your thoughts,
nor are your ways my ways, says the Lord.
For as the heavens are higher than the earth,
so are my ways higher than your ways
and my thoughts than your thoughts."
ISAIAH 55:8-9 NRSV

If you stop to think about it, most of our conversations are made up of a dialogue of various opinions. We talk about the facts, for sure, but the meaningful stuff comes when we start to influence those facts with our own sentiments.

There's nothing wrong with searching for meaning in situations and trying to make sense of the complexities of life. It's possible that the quest for understanding is an integral part of our human nature. However, we ultimately need to surrender our understanding and opinions to God's truth.

In the context of this scripture, God is speaking specifically about his mercy for his people.

> *Are there certain "ways of God" that you just can't make sense of in your life? Be encouraged to surrender your thoughts in order to trust his.*

God, I admit there are ways of yours that I simply cannot understand. I know I need to trust your Word that says your ways and thoughts are higher than mine. Help me not to be offended by your ways.

In the Little Things

Those who know your name trust in you,
for you, O Lord, do not abandon those
who search for you.
PSALM 9:10 NLT

It feels easier to trust God in the big moments, the desperate moments. But what about the everyday moments? The times that we grab hold of control and want to do it all ourselves. In those moments, we can press into him without restraint.

God has given us a huge gift in his faithful nature. He promises us things and sticks to those promises without fail. How beautiful is this God! He will give you a path to confidently walk on if all you do is trust him.

Let go, cry out to him, ask him to carry you. And he will. The everyday moments that might feel crooked will be straightened. He will carry you as he promises. Spend some time with your trustworthy God and thank him for never failing you.

> *Where do you have the most difficulty trusting God? Practice letting go in those moments. Trust him.*

Jesus, thank you for being my good shepherd. Help me to seek out your ways today, in all those everyday decisions. I know you don't need to tell me what exactly to do, but help me to be like you so I reflect your nature to others around me. Help me to trust you with what you are doing in my life right now.

Roots

"They will be like a tree planted by the water
that sends out its roots by the stream.
It does not fear when heat comes;
its leaves are always green.
It has no worries in a year of drought
and never fails to bear fruit."
JEREMIAH 17:8 NIV

Have you ever tried to nurture a plant in a pot? It can flourish with persistent watering, moving it to the right temperature and light, and pruning it when it gets too big. Usually it grows straight up since the pot restricts the roots from growing too wide. Up and up it grows. But if you forget about it for a while, not caring for it the way it was designed to be cared for, it can start to brown, wither, and eventually, it will die.

Roots. They make all the difference in health. Roots take shape underground, where you can't see. Often roots show the true health of anything we examine. We should have deep roots in our heart's devotion to God. Deep doesn't mean a long history; it means that what happens in our homes, our hearts, and our relationships are nourishing and pleasing to God.

Take the time today to ask God for roots that come alive. When you feel you're getting a little brown or wilted, just go to the caretaker and start again. Each time you do, your roots grow a little stronger.

> *Where is your heart health today, spiritually speaking? Do you need persistent watering and nourishment?*

Father, strengthen me now as I come to sit and drink of all that you have to give. Let your words help my roots grow deeper and keep me strong so that I am not thrown around by the wind. Thank you that I carry your love and your grace in my heart and that this keeps me grounded with a deeper understanding of who you are.

God's Ear

I love the LORD, for he heard my voice;
he heard my cry for mercy.
Because he turned his ear to me,
I will call on him as long as I live.
Then I called on the name of the LORD:
"LORD, save me!"
PSALM 116: 1-4 NIV

God hears you. Whether you are shouting praises of thanksgiving, crying tears of mourning, or singing phrases of glory, God hears. He listens. He does not abandon or ignore.

Some days you might not feel worthy of sitting in God's presence. But you are here now. He is a beautiful, caring God who takes us as sinners and holds our hand as we walk the path to salvation. He protects us, encourages us, and gives us salvation!

He hears your voice. He hears your heart. He hears your shouts, your whispers, and your thoughts. Sometimes this seems scary; we feel like we have to perform. That is a lie. Do not believe it. God takes us as we are, where we are. We don't have to filter, pretend, or please. He meets us, loves us, accepts us just as we are in this moment. Remember this truth today, so your soul can rest in his goodness.

Do you believe God hears you?
What do you want to tell him right now?

God, turn your ear toward me today. I have a lot of questions, a lot of decisions to make, and I need your help. Some days I feel like I am drowning and I need saving. I need you to gently whisper into my ear: you are gracious, you are righteous, you are full of compassion. You protect me, save me, and give me rest. You are a good Father.

A Heart for Others

By the grace given to me I say to everyone among you not to think of himself more highly than he ought to think, but to think with sober judgment, each according to the measure of faith that God has assigned.
ROMANS 12:3 ESV

Have you ever felt like you were split-second judged? You had an encounter, it didn't go as planned, and immediately you felt less than ideal. We desire grace for ourselves when we are having a "bad day," but it's so easy to forget to extend that same grace to others. Maybe we've done it for so long that we don't even realize we are doing it.

Do you go about your day with grace in your heart? It can be hard when people are irritating or foolish to not hold judgement over them. But here is what we need to remember: we are the same.

Reflect on the people in your life and your heart toward them. Ask God to give you eyes to see them as he does. We are children of the Most High God, precious, beautifully made in his image. We belong to Jesus. Ask God to give you a heart to see others for who they are and remember they are nothing less than you are.

Have you had a recent encounter where you've judged someone or haven't extended grace?

God, I so easily fall into the trap of comparison, thinking of everyone else's faults before my own. Let me see others around me with a heart of grace, and acknowledge that I am no better than anyone else. You love us all the same. I know I can be judgmental at times and I ask for forgiveness if this has been my heart toward anyone lately. Give me a good perspective so I can be full of love for others.

Peace like a River

"I am the Lord your God,
who teaches you what is best for you,
who directs you in the way you should go.
If only you had paid attention to my commands,
your peace would have been like a river,
your well-being like the waves of the sea."
ISAIAH 48:17-18 NIV

Where do you usually go to find peace? Is there a certain place? A certain person? One of the greatest gifts of God is his undeniable, unfathomable peace. It is a deep well that comes with knowing and experiencing Jesus' love.

Grasp how deep his well runs. Lasting peace and joy does not come in the world or people around you. No matter where you are, where you are going, and whatever you might be experiencing, his peace is greater.

Although some things in life can be comforting, the true, transforming, and powerful peace only comes from your heavenly Father. And oh, how he loves it when you come to his well.

> *Where do you usually turn for peace? Have you experienced the indescribable peace of God?*

God, I know that today will get busy. My days are full of all kinds of things and I thank you for the blessings of children, work, study, and whatever else I am involved in. Fill me up during the day, Lord. As I dwell in your presence that is ever near, I ask for your strength to course through me like a mighty river. I drink of your peace and presence. Refresh my soul.

New Every Morning

Because of the LORD's great love, we are not consumed,
for his compassions never fail.
They are new every morning;
great is your faithfulness.
LAMENTATIONS 3:22-23 NIV

Some days it is good to reflect on exactly what God has saved us from. As a nation, Israel knew what it was to fail God time and time again. They rebelled against him and they deserved punishment; yet, God chose to redeem them, over and over again. His love for his people compelled him to show mercy.

We are not unlike the Israelites in our rebellion and turning away from God's purposes. We are also not unlike the Israelites in that God has incredible compassion for us. In sending his Son, Jesus Christ, God proved once and for all that his compassion will never fail.

Why does God's compassion have to appear new every morning? Because we can barely go a day without failing. We need to be reminded of God's faithfulness so that we can turn toward him, daily.

Did you fail God yesterday, or today?
His mercy endures!

Thank you, Father, for your compassion every single morning. I confess my sin and I am ready to start the day new.

Just Rest

The Lord will give strength to His people;
The Lord will bless His people with peace.
PSALM 29:11 NKJV

Picture a season in your life where you were knee-deep in busyness, swallowed in sadness, or buried in exhaustion. Picture that season and how you looked, acted, reacted, and survived. Now picture Jesus. See his face, feel his warmth, envision his smile.

Picture yourself back in that same tiresome season, sitting on a chair in your house, desiring to spend time with God but being so extremely tired that you couldn't find the strength. These are the times when he longs to draw near.

Do you feel weary after a long day? Perhaps you deal with children, or are working toward an important deadline for work or study. It's hard to feel peace when you are so busy and yet so tired. Give your days to the Lord. Take moments to rest. Allow his peace to settle on your heart and give you the strength you need.

Have you encountered a moment with Jesus where you understood more fully that he gets you to your very core? He knows your heart. He knows when your soul needs rest.

God, I know what it is like to be weary and weak. Thank you that you have always been my strength and that you will be it again today. I need rest. I need you to fill this tired mind and heart with your presence. Be my strength, and bless me with your peace.

Change of Season

"Be strong and courageous, and act; do not fear nor be dismayed, for the Lord God, my God, is with you. He will not fail you nor forsake you until all the work for the service of the house of the Lord is finished."

1 CHRONICLES 28:20 NASB

Seasons can be challenging. They require bravery, obedience, dedication, and sometimes total upheaval of everything comfortable in our lives. If we feel that impending corner of a seasonal shift in our hearts, it usually means God is preparing us for something different—a change.

You will, undoubtedly, have various seasons in your life: seasons of longing and contentment, seasons of discouragement and joy, seasons of more and less. Being a grown-up means stretching into new ways of living, and this usually doesn't happen until the season hits.

In those seasons of life, the one who won't change, won't back down, and won't leave us stranded is our heavenly Father. Be brave! God will not move you into something without giving you the grace you need to make it through.

> *Do you see an impending season change approaching? How does it make you feel?*

Father God, thank you for this season of my life. Please give me the courage to know that you are with me now and whatever season you may call me forward into. If this is where you want me right now, then sustain me and help me to be content. If you are calling me to move forward, then help me to be brave, knowing that you are with me.